11/05

COLOMBIA
in Pictures

Tom Streissguth

Lerner Publications Company

Contents

Website address: www.lernerbooks.com

Lerner Publications Company
A division of Lerner Publishing Group
241 First Avenue North
Minneapolis, MN 55401 U.S.A.

web enhanced @ www.vgsbooks.com

Library of Congress Cataloging-in-Publication Data

Streissguth, Thomas, 1958–
    Colombia in pictures / by Tom Streissguth.
        p. cm. – (Visual geography series)
    Summary: Text and illustrations present detailed information on the geography, history and
government, economy, people, cultural life and society of traditional and modern Colombia.
    Includes bibliographical references and index.
    ISBN. 0-8225-0933-4 (lib. bdg. : alk. paper)
    1. Colombia. [1. Colombia.] I. Title. II. Visual geography series (Minneapolis, MN)
F2258.S85 2004
986.1—dc22   2003015414

Manufactured in the United States of America
1 2 3 4 5 6 - JR - 09 08 07 06 05 04

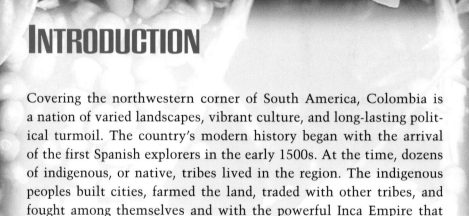

INTRODUCTION

Covering the northwestern corner of South America, Colombia is a nation of varied landscapes, vibrant culture, and long-lasting political turmoil. The country's modern history began with the arrival of the first Spanish explorers in the early 1500s. At the time, dozens of indigenous, or native, tribes lived in the region. The indigenous peoples built cities, farmed the land, traded with other tribes, and fought among themselves and with the powerful Inca Empire that lay to the south.

In search of the legendary El Dorado, a city of gold, Spanish conquistadors (conquerors) marched from Colombia's Pacific and Caribbean coasts into the indigenous homelands. The conquistadors established a colonial state under Spanish rule. The Spanish colonists imposed a new culture, religion, and economic system and wiped out entire indigenous societies through warfare and disease.

For 250 years after the Spanish arrived, the city of Bogotá was the capital of New Granada, a territory that included present-day

Colombia, Panama, Venezuela, and Ecuador. Soon after New Granada won independence from Spain in 1819, Venezuela and Ecuador broke from Colombia. In 1903 Colombia lost control of Panama as an independence movement supported by the United States took hold.

Throughout Colombia's history as an independent nation, its people have endured years of unrest and civil war as the two main political factions—Liberals and Conservatives—vied for power. Sometimes Colombia's leaders manage to hammer out a truce, and citizens can draw on a wealth of natural resources and modernized industry to improve their health, education, and standard of living. Such a period of growth and improvement occurred in the late twentieth century, when Colombia prospered from strong exports and farm production. These achievements allowed Colombia to avoid problems such as price inflation, widespread unemployment, and labor strife, which marked the history of many other countries in Central and South America.

But Colombia has not achieved peace. The government must deal with large groups of armed rebels in the countryside. Seeking to disrupt public order and the government, these leftist guerrilla fighters carry out assassinations, bombings, kidnappings, and other violent acts. Adding to the violence are right-wing paramilitary armies that are determined to bring down the rebels. Both the leftist guerrillas and the right-wing paramilitaries earn much of their money from drug trafficking. Illegal drug processing and distribution are deeply entrenched problems in Colombia. For decades this drug traffic has undermined the country's political and social institutions and contributed to the violence.

The struggle continues in Colombia to bring opposing leaders and factions to some kind of agreement and achieve political stability. Discouraged by the government's failure to resolve the civil war and disillusioned by the unfulfilled promises of President Andres Pastrana, many voters stayed away from the polls during recent elections. Those who did vote gave Conservative party member Alvaro Uribe a solid majority and the presidency. But many people have lost hope that their government will be able to solve the country's ongoing problems. Although Colombia has the potential to become an economic leader in South America, it must first achieve peace and stability within its own borders.

THE LAND

The Republic of Colombia lies in the northwestern corner of South America, linking the continent with Central America. Colombia is the fourth largest country in South America, after Brazil, Argentina, and Peru. Neighboring countries include Ecuador to the southwest, Peru to the south, Brazil to the east and southeast, and Venezuela to the northeast. In the northwest, a strip of Panama divides Colombia's Caribbean coast, which extends for about 1,000 miles (1,600 kilometers), and the 800-mile (1,300-km) coastline along the Pacific Ocean. The San Andrés y Providencia archipelago, a group of islands claimed by Colombia, lies 400 miles (650 km) northwest of the mainland in the eastern Caribbean. Colombia covers 440,831 square miles (1,141,748 square km), about three times the area of Montana.

◉ The Andean Highlands

Three mountain ranges, forming the northern end of the Andes Mountains, run through western Colombia. Formed by the collision of

three plates within the earth's crust, the Andean *cordilleras* (ranges) include several active volcanoes—Galeras, Huila, and Ruiz, which erupted in 1985 and destroyed the town of Armero. Colombia also is jolted by frequent earthquakes. In 1999 a strong quake damaged many cities and towns in the Andes region.

The Cordillera Occidental, or western range, is the lowest of the three ranges. It runs north and south about 50 miles (80 km) from the Pacific coast. The highest point in this range, Cerro Tamaná, reaches 13,780 feet (4,200 meters). Just to the north, the range divides into three smaller highlands, known as the Abibe, San Jerónimo, and Ayapel mountains. The fertile Cauca River Valley, long the site of important towns and settlements, divides the Cordillera Occidental from the Cordillera Central. The Cordillera Central is Colombia's highest mountain range, with an average elevation of 10,000 feet (3,048 m).

The Magdalena River, the longest in Colombia, divides the Cordillera Central and the Cordillera Oriental, or eastern range. At the

The Magdalena River, one of Colombia's largest and most heavily traveled waterways, begins in the Andes and empties into the Caribbean Sea near Barranquilla in the north.

northern limits of the Cordillera Oriental, the peak of Alto Ritacuva rises 18,021 feet (5,493 m). In the far north, the Sierra Nevada de Santa Marta range rises just south of the Caribbean coast. Within this range lies the country's highest point, Pico Cristóbal Colón (also known as Bolívar Peak), at 18,947 feet (5,775 m). To the east, the hot desert of La Guajira Peninsula, which lies partly in Colombia and partly in Venezuela, extends into the Caribbean.

The Llanos

The eastern half of Colombia is dominated by flat grasslands and forested plains known as the Llanos. A small range of hills, the Sierra de la Macarena, rises at the western edge of the Llanos. In the southeast is a region of tropical rain forest known as the *selva.* Remote and inaccessible in many parts,

A rancher rounds up his cattle in the Llanos region.

CARIBBEAN SEA

La Guajira
Peninsula

Pico Cristóbal
Colón ▲

SIERRA NEVADA
DE SANTA MARTA

Gulf of
Urabá

PANAMA

VENEZUELA

Sirú River

Cauca River

SAN JERÓNIMO
MTNS.

Darien
Gap

AYAPEL MTNS.

ABIBE MTNS.

Magdalena River

Arauca River

Alto Ritacuva ▲

CHOCÓ

CORDILLERA OCCIDENTAL

Cauca
River
Valley

CORDILLERA CENTRAL

Magdalena River Valley

CORDILLERA ORIENTAL

Meta River

Orinoco River

PACIFIC

OCEAN

San Juan R.

Cerro
Tamaná ▲

▲ Ruiz

Lake
Guatávita

L L A N O S

Dagua
River

CORDILLERA

Cauca
River

Huila ▲

SIERRA DE LA
MACARENA

Patía R.

A N D E S

Vaupés River

Mira R.

Galeras ▲

Equator

Caquetá River

ECUADOR

Putumayo River

BRAZIL

PERU

Amazon River

Colombia

Feet	Meters	
13124+	4000+	
9843	3000	Mountains
6582	2000	Uplands
3281	1000	
1640	500	Lowlands

Elevation

N

———— International border
▲ Mountain peak
▲ Volcano

0   200 Miles

0   200 KM

CARIBBEAN SEA

SAN ANDRÉS
Y PROVIDENCIA
ISLANDS

NICARAGUA

PACIFIC
OCEAN

COLOMBIA

0   250 Miles
0   250 KM

THE DANGEROUS DARIEN GAP

The Pan-American Highway stretches some 17,000 miles (27,350 km) from the southern tip of South America all the way to Alaska—with only a single break. About 54 miles (90 km) of the highway have not been completed. The unfinished stretch runs through the Darien Gap, the region separating Central America and South America, along the border between Panama and Colombia. The Darien Gap is a dangerous area of dense rain forest, roadless hills and valleys, and frequent combat between guerrilla and paramilitary forces. Many winding rivers in the area must be either crossed or used as treacherous transportation routes. Starting in 1984, U.S. explorer Loren Upton made the very first all-land crossing of the Darien Gap, traveling in a 1966 jeep. The 125-mile (200-km) journey took 741 days—more than two years.

the Llanos remain home to indigenous groups who still live by traditional hunting and gathering.

The low-lying Chocó, a hot, humid region of dense rain forest, mangrove swamps, and extremely heavy rainfall, stretches along the Pacific coast. The heavy rains create waterfalls and rapidly flowing rivers that tumble westward into the sea. The region has few roads or towns of any size, very little flat land for growing crops, and limited natural resources. The Pan-American Highway, which was planned to link South, Central, and North America, does not cut through the northern Chocó. Environmental groups striving to preserve the Chocó forest have prevented construction of the highway in the region.

◉ Rivers

The center of a vital agricultural area, the Magdalena River begins in the Andes Mountains of southern Colombia. It flows north between the Cordillera Central and the Cordillera Oriental, finally emptying into the Caribbean Sea near the city of Barranquilla. The Magdalena Valley is the site of several major cities and has long been a center of Colombian agriculture. The Cauca River, the Magdalena's major tributary, runs a parallel northerly course through the Cauca Valley.

In northeastern Colombia, the Meta and Arauca rivers flow east across the border with Venezuela before emptying into the Orinoco River. In the southeast, the Vaupés, Caquetá, and Putumayo rivers all reach the Amazon, South America's major river, which forms a short segment of the southeastern border of Colombia with Peru. In western Colombia, a series of short, rapid rivers, including the San Juan,

Dagua, Patía, and Mira, tumble into the Pacific Ocean from their sources high in the Cordillera Occidental.

◉ Climate

Because Colombia lies close to the equator, where seasons and weather do not change much, the country's climate varies more by elevation than by location. Temperatures decrease as altitude increases. Elevations below about 3,000 feet (914 m) are known as the *tierra caliente,* or "hot land." The middle elevations are *tierra templada* ("moderate land"), and the highest zone, above 6,500 feet (1,980 m), is the *tierra fría* ("cold land"). In the highest reaches of the Andes, snow and ice blanket the mountainsides year-round.

Precipitation is heaviest in the Magdalena Valley and the tropical forests of eastern Colombia, where more than 100 inches (250 centimeters) of rain fall in a typical year. In the upper Magdalena Valley and the northern lowlands, a dry season begins in November and continues through early spring, while the wet season runs from May to October. Rainfall averages 50 to 75 inches (125 to 190 cm) per year in these regions. The area along the Caribbean coast is the driest, hottest part of the country, with short rainy seasons in spring and fall. The temperature in this region averages about 80°F (27°C) year-round. The Guajira Peninsula receives the least amount of rain in Colombia.

◉ Flora and Fauna

With its diverse geography and climates, Colombia has a rich variety of plant and animal life. In the jungles that cover the remote reaches of the Andes, a great range of vegetation remains undisturbed by commercial development and lumbering. Forest plants include bamboo trees, bromeliads, ivory nut trees, and hundreds of species of lianas (hanging vines). The higher altitudes, known as the *páramos,* are home to alpine vegetation, such as lichens and mosses, as well as a tall plant called the *frailejón* ("tall friar"). More than three thousand species of orchids grow

Alpine plants such as the **frailejón** grow in Colombia's mountainous regions.

throughout Colombia. These plants get their nutrients from air rather than soil and depend on moisture from rain and humidity to survive. Plants that process water and nutrients in this way are called epiphytes.

Colombia's natural fauna include large cats such as the puma and jaguar, as well as smaller ocelots, which live in remote regions and in the rain forests. Monkeys, peccaries (a mammal related to the pig), tapirs, deer, and large rodents such as the capybara live in the tropical forests and low-

Capybara

lands. Colombian river creatures include eels, crocodiles, piranhas, and a big freshwater fish called the bocachica. Turtles, snakes, and many large and small lizards can be found throughout the country. Colombia also is home to a great variety of birds, including condors, macaws, toucans, and parrots.

◯ Natural Resources

Europeans came to Colombia in search of gold, and the theft of gold ore and artifacts helped fuel the colonial-era economy. In modern times,

AMAZON RIVER DOLPHINS

Two different dolphin species inhabit the Amazon River and its tributaries. The boto dolphin, *Inia geoffrensis*, grows nearly 10 feet (3 m) long and is pale pink. The tucuxi dolphin, *Sotalia fluviatilis*, is smaller, averaging 5 feet (1.5 m) long—but it eats 11 pounds (5 kilograms) of fish every day!

A tucuxi dolphin splashes in the Orinoco River. Visit vgsbooks.com to learn more about Colombia's dolphins and other wildlife.

Colombia profits from reserves of fossil fuels, including coal, petroleum, and natural gas. Mineral resources include iron ore, nickel, gold, and a large deposit of copper that was discovered in the 1970s in the western department (region) of Antioquia. Large reserves of bauxite, the mineral used in processing aluminum, are also found in Colombia. Emeralds from Colombian lakes, rivers, and hillsides are sold all over the world.

About 5 percent of the land in Colombia is suitable for farming, with especially fertile tracts in the Magdalena and Cauca valleys. The country's waterways are used for hydropower projects that have provided abundant energy to cities and industry.

Environmental Issues

Much of Colombia's natural vegetation has been destroyed or permanently altered as people have settled the land and cleared forests. Although mining and agriculture are important to the Colombian economy, these activities have degraded the natural environment.

Rain forest

Mining pollutes waterways and hillsides, while farming requires that trees be cleared for pastures and crops. Due to clearing and burning, the rain forest is disappearing at the rate of 2,500 square miles (6,500 sq. km) a year, allowing heavy rainfall to wash away the fertile topsoil.

The Colombian government has attempted to curb destruction of the rain forest but lacks adequate resources to meet this challenge. In some rural regions dominated by civil conflict and guerrilla warfare, the government has no authority at all. In the twentieth century, Colombia set aside a large network of natural preserves, including thirty-three national parks, six sanctuaries, and two reserves. Many parks and reserves, however, represent little more than lines on a government map, as these places do not have facilities in place for visitors. There is no guarantee that the natural ecosystems will be preserved in these areas.

Cities

BOGOTÁ Founded as Santafé de Bogotá, this capital city of seven million people sprawls across the Sabana de Bogotá, a highland plain that was once home to the Muisca Indians. The city is the hub of the Cundinamarca Department in central Colombia. With a base elevation of 8,660 feet (2,640 m), Bogotá has spread to the foothills of the surrounding mountains.

Bogotá, Colombia's capital, is a large and expanding urban center. The city lies nearly 2 miles (3 km) above sea level, and walking its streets can cause altitude sickness in those unused to the thin atmosphere.

In April 1538, the Spanish explorer Gonzalo Jiménez de Quesada founded a settlement on the site of Bacatá, the Muisca capital. During the colonial period, the town grew as a central staging point for expeditions into the Andes and the Llanos. In 1717 Santafé de Bogotá became the capital of the Viceroyalty of New Granada, a Spanish colony. When Colombia became an independent country, Bogotá remained the capital. But it did not grow rapidly until the 1940s, when new industries attracted thousands of rural laborers to the city. In 1948 Bogotá suffered through a period of political violence known as the *bogotazo*. This conflict destroyed many of the city's older buildings.

Since then the city has become a chaotic jumble of skyscrapers, traffic-jammed boulevards, wealthy residential neighborhoods, and vast poor neighborhoods, or barrios, where migrants from the countryside struggle to survive. An important commercial and cultural center, Bogotá has Colombia's largest banks, hundreds of major companies, and more than thirty universities. The city is home to about one-sixth of Colombia's population, and it produces about the same proportion of the nation's goods and services.

MEDELLÍN is the capital of the Antioquia Department and lies along the Medellín River in the Aburrá Valley of the Cordillera Central.

The city, which has a population of two million people, was established in 1616 by Jewish refugees fleeing religious persecution in Europe. Medellín prospered, thanks to its citizens' hard work and its valuable natural resources, including gold. Modern industries include glassmaking, textile production, and medical services.

Medellín gained an unsavory reputation during the 1980s as the home of the Medellín drug cartel, a powerful and violent criminal organization. After a government crackdown in the 1990s led to the capture of the cartel's principal leaders, drug-related violence ebbed in Medellín. The center of the illegal drug trade moved to the smaller city of Cali to the south.

The people of Medellín enjoy the best public services in Colombia, including modern bus and subway systems as well as

With its temperate climate, vibrant artistic scene, active sports culture, and famed annual flower festival, Medellín has earned the nickname "city of eternal spring."

updated water, sewage, and electricity networks. The city has a reputation for orderliness and cleanliness, and it provides the nation's leading health and education services.

Many Colombians consider Medellín the cultural capital of the nation. The city is famous as the birthplace of painter Fernando Botero, and it boasts dozens of museums, art galleries, concert halls, and theaters. Thriving universities, including the University of Antioquia, attract students to Medellín from all over the country.

CALI, with a population of 2.1 million, lies near the Pacific Coast in the Valle del Cauca Department in west-central Colombia. A dry, sunny climate and a dramatic landscape, bordered by two mountain ranges, add to Cali's reputation as a fine place to live and work.

Cali was founded in 1536 by Sebastián de Belalcázar after he had a falling-out with his commander Francisco Pizarro, a Spanish explorer. Colonial landowners made use of the area's fertile soil to raise sugarcane, which has remained the economic lifeblood of the Cauca Valley ever since. The city of Cali boomed in the mid-twentieth century with the growth of modern agricultural and manufacturing industries. The city government made efforts to clean up the Río Cali, a once-stagnant and polluted stream that runs through the center of the city, and also built a modern subway system.

Cali is known for its Pan-American Sports Complex, built in 1971, and La Plaza de Toros de Cañaveralejo, the largest bullring in Colombia. The *caleños,* or people of Cali, are also proud of their city as the birthplace and capital of salsa music, the rhythmic dance music that swept Latin America and the Caribbean in the late twentieth century.

Fans cheer wildly at **La Plaza de Toros de Cañaveralejo in Cali.** The sport of bullfighting originated in Spain and has taken hold in Colombia and many other Spanish-speaking countries.

Cartagena's intact walled quarter and colonial architecture draw many tourists.

OTHER CITIES The largest cities on Colombia's Caribbean coast are Barranquilla (population 1.3 million) and Cartagena (population 800,000). Barranquilla is famous for its annual carnival. For several days each spring, townspeople and visitors mingle in the crowded streets, enjoying music, food, and dancing. Cartagena is a popular tourist destination and is well known for the walls that surround the city's old quarter. The people of Cartagena take pride in the fact that their city was the first in Colombia to declare independence, an event that the entire nation celebrates as a public holiday.

For links to websites where you can find out more about the cities of Colombia—such as Bogotá, Medellín, Cali, Barranquilla, and Cartagena—including climate information and weather forecasts, go to vgsbooks.com.

HISTORY AND GOVERNMENT

The "pre-Columbian" population of Colombia—the groups of people who lived in the region before the arrival of Europeans—settled in the Cauca River Valley, the Cordillera Central, and the high plateaus of the Cordillera Oriental range. Historians have dated the earliest human settlements in the region to about 20,000 B.C. New waves of Mesoamericans—indigenous peoples of Central America—arrived between 1200 and 500 B.C., giving rise to the distinct cultural groups that dominated the river valleys and the Caribbean coast.

Indigenous Civilizations

The Chibcha people, who came from Central America in about 400 B.C., lived in scattered villages throughout the region. The Chibcha farmed the land, developed irrigation systems, mined emeralds and salt, and built an extensive network of roads and suspension bridges. Some historians have estimated that the Chibcha population reached a peak of one million.

The Tayrona people lived along the Caribbean coast and in the Sierra
Nevada de Santa Marta. They lived by fishing and by trading with other
tribes. Skilled engineers and architects, the Tayrona built paved roads,
aqueducts, and large public plazas. But their wealth also attracted inva-
sions of the Carib people, who lived on islands in the Caribbean Sea, and
of Spanish conquerors starting in the early sixteenth century. The remains
of a major Tayrona settlement, known as La Ciudad Perdida, or "lost
city," were discovered in 1975. Carefully planned and laid out, La Ciudad
Perdida encompasses hundreds of stone terraces set on a steep hillside.

The Sinú people lived to the southwest of the Tayrona, near the
mouth of the Sinú River on the Caribbean coast. The Quimbaya people
farmed the lowlands along the Cauca River in western Colombia. The
Quimbaya crafted beautiful ornaments and statues from the gold they
found along the hillsides and in riverbeds.

The Muisca people, who lived in the valleys around present-day
Bogotá, traded gold, emeralds, textiles, ceramics, and food. They also

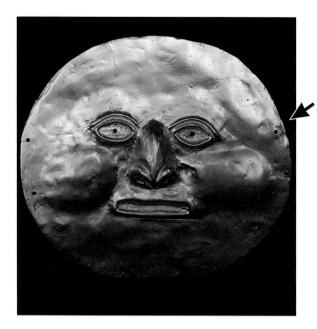

Some of the early peoples who inhabited Colombia crafted spectacular jewelry, weapons, vessels, and masks out of gold. **This mask,** made by the Calima people, is similar to pieces created by the Muisca.

worked gold into spectacular jewelry and statues. With their fertile land and other resources, the Muisca were one of the wealthiest and most powerful indigenous groups in Colombia by the early 1500s, the time of the first arrivals from Europe on the Caribbean coast of South America.

European Contact

Compared with most other places in South America, Colombia abounded in gold. This valuable metal drew Europeans to the Caribbean and Pacific shores of Colombia, culminating in a chaotic period of violence and conquest.

The first European to sight Colombia was a colleague of Christopher Columbus named Alonso de Ojeda, who accompanied Columbus on his second voyage to the Americas in the fall of 1493. Ojeda sailed along the Guajira Peninsula in 1499. The explorers Rodrigo de Bastidas and Juan de la Cosa surveyed Colombia's Caribbean coastline in 1500 and 1501. In search of treasure and slaves, de la Cosa returned to Colombia in 1505, raiding villages along the banks of the Sinú River.

In 1508 Ojeda and de la Cosa joined forces and arrived at present-day Cartagena. They were driven back by indigenous warriors, who killed de la Cosa. Ojeda continued into the interior, where he encountered the Tayrona people. Ojeda and other Spanish explorers saw that the Tayrona and other tribes possessed a wealth of gold artwork and jewelry. These discoveries originated the myth of "El Dorado"—a land rich in gold and precious jewelry. In fact, much of the gold had been obtained as trade goods from Central America and the Inca Empire to the south. But the drive to capture these mythical riches inspired many Spanish expeditions to Colombia.

Ojeda explored the Sierra Nevada de Santa Marta and continued as far west as the Gulf of Urabá, near the southern limit of the Isthmus of Panama. In 1510 Ojeda founded San Sebastían de Urabá, the first Spanish settlement in Colombia. Soon afterward, he founded another settlement on the Gulf of Urabá. But he was wounded by a poisoned arrow and fled for the island of Hispaniola, where he died in 1515.

Over the next several years, Spanish explorers established several settlements in Colombia. But their isolated towns and farms came under constant attack by local indigenous groups. None of the towns endured until Santa Marta was founded in 1525 by Rodrigo de Bastidas. The Spanish used this settlement on the Caribbean coast as a base to explore the Sierra Nevada de Santa Marta. They made their way across the forbidding mountains and steep valleys and fought the Chibcha and other indigenous peoples of the Andean highlands.

EL DORADO

The famous El Dorado myth originated with the Muisca tribe. Believing in the powers of a sacred lake, the people threw offerings into the waters of Laguna de Guatavita. The story of a city of riches inspired a series of Spanish expeditions into Colombia in the early 1500s. In 1580 explorers discovered the emerald-colored lake north of Bogotá. They drained the lake by forcing thousands of Indians to dig a canal through a mountainside, but the Spaniards found little gold. Over time, heavy rains refilled the lake. In 1904 a British company drained the lake again. Gold-hunting expeditions continued at the lake until 1965, when Colombia made the Laguna de Guatavita a protected national monument.

In 1533 the Spaniard Pedro de Heredia founded the city of Cartagena, which became an important Spanish trading port on the Caribbean Sea. Soon afterward, Sebastián de Belalcázar began surveying Colombia from the Pacific coast, founding the towns of Popayán and Cali. In 1538 Gonzalo Jiménez de Quesada conquered the Chibcha people of the Magdalena River Valley. The conquistadors destroyed native villages and homes and built new Christian churches. The most important Chibcha town, Bogotá, became the capital of the new Spanish colony in 1539.

The conquest of the Chibcha and other indigenous tribes was carried out with great violence. Chiefs and tribal leaders were tortured and killed, and the Spaniards enslaved millions of people to work on the land and in the mines of the new European colony. Many indigenous societies simply disappeared through war and disease, while the survivors were forced to convert to Christianity. The Spanish considered religious conversion a crucial part of their mission in the New World. As a result, the culture of the original inhabitants was overwhelmed by the institutions—religious, economic, and political—brought from Europe.

◉ The Audiencia

In 1549 Jiménez de Quesada established the Audiencia of New Granada. New Granada was a department, which encompassed what is now Colombia, within the Viceroyalty of Peru, a huge domain covering all of South America except for Brazil and Venezuela. The viceroyalty was a Spanish colony governed by a viceroy, a leader appointed by the king of Spain. The *audiencia* was a council that managed the administrative and judicial affairs of the department. In the early years of the new colony, few Spaniards were willing to make the long and risky sea voyage to this distant outpost of the kingdom. Poor roads and attacks by indigenous tribes also slowed settlement.

Gradually, however, a steadily growing population of colonists created a stable society. Farming and gold mining were the mainstays of the colonial economy. To solve the problem of a labor shortage in the colony, the Spanish government created the *encomienda* system. The king granted parcels of land called encomiendas to settlers, who in turn forced the indigenous population to work for them. Slave traders also brought captive Africans to the Caribbean coast, where busy slave markets provided labor for gold mines and the encomiendas.

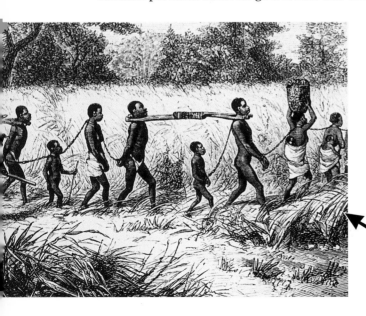

Slaves captured in Africa were shipped to destinations throughout North and South America, including Colombia.

Catholic missionaries rest against a church wall overlooking Cartagena. The Roman Catholic Church had immense influence over Colombian life during the 1500s.

The Roman Catholic Church dominated culture and education in the viceroyalty. The Church operated the few existing schools, worked to convert the indigenous tribes to Catholicism, and played an important role in government. Catholic clergy presided at baptisms, funerals, festivals, and weddings.

As the various groups in the colony—European settlers, indigenous peoples, and African slaves—began to marry and have families, they created a unique Colombian ethnic mix. People of mixed European and indigenous heritage were referred to as *mestizos,* while those who were a mix of African and Spanish parentage were called *mulatos.*

Tensions in the Colony

The king of Spain appointed Juan de Borja, the conqueror of the Pijaos tribe of the Cordillera Central, as president of the Audiencia of New Granada in 1605. Borja, who ruled until 1628, brought new areas under the control of the audiencia and carried out military campaigns against indigenous groups who were still resisting rule by the Spanish. The audiencia minted silver coins, which helped colonists buy, sell, and trade their goods with each other and the outside world. In 1637 the presidency passed into the hands of Spanish nobles, who were weak, corrupt political leaders. New settlement in the viceroyalty declined through the late 1600s, and many colonists living in the poorest and most isolated regions simply abandoned their towns.

The viceroyalty entered a period of ongoing political instability in the early 1700s. Governors who ruled the outlying regions defied the administration in Bogotá. The ports of New Granada came under attack by the French, while a new colony of Scottish settlers—with a very different language, religion, culture, and outlook—established themselves

THE COLONIAL TOWN

The towns founded by colonists in Colombia followed a strict plan, dictated by the king's government in Spain. Towns had to include a central plaza, with the four sides facing the main points of the compass. One or more sides of the plaza were supposed to have arcades (covered walkways) for the convenience of visiting traders, who would be able to display their goods in a public yet sheltered place. The streets ran north-south and east-west in a grid pattern. Streets in one direction were named *calles*, and those in the other were *carreras*. Builders were supposed to place the town church away from the central plaza, if possible on a high point of ground that was easy to see. To this day, many of Colombia's towns still have the central plaza and grid street pattern that originated in colonial times.

at Darien, near the Isthmus of Panama. The audiencia did not have the resources to defend its ports and coastline. Trade was declining, and pirates hijacked shipments of gold and diverted them to Spain's European rivals, who were prohibited from trading directly with Spanish colonies.

A labor shortage hurt many rural landowners, who were unable to harvest crops such as wheat and sugarcane. As the encomienda system declined, whites and mestizos in search of work set up smaller farming estates, while manufacturing businesses sprang up in the growing colonial towns. Most of the people who owned and operated these industries were criollos, or Spaniards who were born in the colony. (Spaniards born in Spain were called *peninsulares*.) Criollos also made up much of the upper class of political leaders and wealthy landowners. They were loyal to the king of Spain but had few economic or cultural ties to the mother country.

In 1717 Spain established the Viceroyalty of New Granada, which included present-day Colombia, Panama, Venezuela, and Ecuador. As the capital of the viceroyalty, Bogotá became one of the most important cities in the Spanish colonial empire. Through the 1700s, trade and settlement increased in the viceroyalty. As New Granada prospered, the administration in Bogotá got stronger. Spain also opened the colony's ports to other European nations, which further improved trade.

But political dissent and a drive for independence went hand in hand with the new prosperity. Many colonists resisted rule by the distant Spanish royalty, who took the viceroyalty's gold and other resources to fill their own treasuries. Landowners and merchants embraced republicanism, or government without a king. They also called for free trade, independence from Spain, and an end to slavery.

They drew inspiration from the United States' colonial revolution against Great Britain and the rebellion in France, which resulted in the overthrow of the French king. Uprisings against Spanish rule began with a rebellion known as the Comunero Revolt in the Santander Province in 1781. The revolt was quickly crushed, however.

○ The Fight for Independence

The independence movement remained poorly organized until 1808, when the French leader Napoléon Bonaparte overthrew the king of Spain. Discontented colonists in New Granada seized their opportunity. Over the next few years, several cities broke away from the Spanish government to establish *cabildos,* or independent regions. In 1810 the city of Cartagena formed a junta, or council, of local nobles to replace the colonial governor. On July 20 of that year, the people of Santafé de Bogotá rose in revolt, an event that modern Colombians celebrate on Independence Day.

In Bogotá the rebel council formed the independent state of Cundinamarca in 1813. But fighting soon erupted between Cundinamarca and other new states within the viceroyalty. In 1814 the Spanish king was restored to power after defeating the French. Seeing an opportunity to reestablish power in Colombia, the Spanish government sent a military expedition to land at Santa Marta. The Spaniards restored their colonial government by force, and hundreds of rebel leaders were arrested and executed.

But the government's harsh repression had the opposite effect on the colonists than the authorities had intended. Instead of dashing colonists' hopes for independence, the crackdown spurred renewed efforts against Spanish rule. The Venezuelan revolutionary leader Simón Bolívar arrived in New Granada in 1812 to fight for the colony's independence. But the provinces would not unite their forces under Bolívar's banner, and he fled New Granada in 1815.

Bolívar had enthusiastically taken up the ideals of the American Revolution and hoped to spark a similar rebellion in the Spanish colonies of South America. In 1816 Bolívar returned from exile in Jamaica to the coast of Venezuela. He fought his way to New Granada and finally defeated the Spanish in the Battle of Boyacá on August 7, 1819. This proved to be the final blow to Spain's rule of New Granada. On December 17, the viceroyalty proclaimed independence as the Republic of Gran Colombia. This new state included

Simón Bolívar

The Battle of Boyacá was the turning point in Colombia's struggle for independence.

Colombia, Peru (north of the Marañón and Amazon rivers), Ecuador, Venezuela, and Panama.

New Constitutions

The new country's leaders were Simón Bolívar as president and army general Francisco de Paula Santander as vice president. These two men and their followers formed two rival political factions, the Conservatives and the Liberals. The Liberals favored weaker central government, freedom of the press, and separation of church and state. They also supported public education and universal suffrage, or the right to vote for all citizens. Supported by wealthy landowners and the Catholic Church, Conservatives strongly favored centralized government, close ties between the government and the church, slavery, and limits on the right to vote. At the Congress of Cúcuta in 1821, political leaders drew up a constitution for Gran Colombia that followed the Conservative philosophy.

The various political groups within the large new nation and the leaders of its far-flung provinces often found themselves at odds with the federal government in Bogotá. Conflict flared over the structure of the government—whether it would have strong central authority over the provinces or whether the provinces would hold most of the political, military, and economic power. In 1826 Venezuela proclaimed its independence from Gran Colombia. In response, Bolívar returned to Colombia from his headquarters in Peru and imposed a harsh dictatorship. This regime inspired even more determined resistance and an attempt on Bolívar's life in 1828. In 1830 both Ecuador and Venezuela successfully broke away from Gran Colombia, and Bolívar died in Santa Marta on December 17 of that year. Santander succeeded him as president of Gran Colombia.

Continued strife between the Conservatives and Liberals brought all-out civil war from 1839 to 1842, a time known as the War of the Supremes. The war ended with the triumph of government forces under General Pedro Alcantara Herrán, who was elected president in 1841. After the war, the government began a series of political and economic reforms under the direction of presidents Tomás Cipriano de Mosquera, who took office in 1845, and his successor, General José Hilario López. They abolished slavery, ended government censorship of the press, and lowered tariffs (import taxes) on foreign goods. An amended constitution in 1853 greatly weakened the central government by passing authority from Bogotá to the regional capitals.

> The coffee plant was first brought to Colombia from the Caribbean in the late 1700s, and Colombian farmers began to export coffee beans beginning in 1834.

Gran Colombia wrote a new constitution in 1863, establishing the United States of Colombia. Known as the Rionegro Constitution, this document further weakened the federal government. The constitution created nine states that had the power to form their own armies, set their own taxes, and decide on their own voting laws.

The Rionegro Constitution led to ongoing instability as states fought among themselves over trade and territory. An economic decline caused by a fall in imports only made the situation worse. Civil war flared again in 1876, and in 1886 President Rafael Núñez denounced the Rionegro Constitution. A new constitution established the Republic of Colombia and replaced the semi-independent states with departments that came under stricter control from Bogotá.

During a period known as the Regeneration, from 1880 to 1895, Colombian leaders launched sweeping economic reforms. The government raised tariffs on imports, established a national bank to issue currency and make loans, and invested directly in new industries. In addition, coffee provided a new source of income for the country. By the end of the nineteenth century, coffee was Colombia's most important export and was driving the national economy.

Coffee was vulnerable to price swings, however, and in the 1890s, when the price of coffee fell, Colombians suffered rising inflation and unemployment. These economic woes contributed to political turmoil. In 1899 tensions between Liberals and Conservatives sparked the War of a Thousand Days, fought by loosely organized but fiercely dedicated

A group of young soldiers stands at attention during the last days of the War of a Thousand Days. Even preteen boys joined in the fighting in this bloody civil war.

groups aligned with the two parties. The civil war lasted until 1902, ravaging the country and killing more than 100,000 combatants and civilians.

Civil Strife and La Violencia

The War of a Thousand Days drastically weakened central authority in Colombia. One consequence was that Panama seceded from the republic in 1903, during construction of the Panama Canal. Completed in 1914, the canal opened a passageway between the Caribbean Sea and the Pacific Ocean. This greatly reduced the time and expense of making the long trip around Cape Horn, at the tip of South America. The canal could have been an economic boon for Colombia if Panama had remained part of Colombia. Instead, the canal was controlled by the United States, which had supported the Panamanian independence movement and financed the building of the canal. In 1921 the United States paid $25 million to Colombia for the loss of Panama, and Colombia formally recognized Panama's independence.

Colombia's economy continued to grow during the 1920s, when taxes on coffee exports brought large sums into the national treasury. New roads and railroads were built, and a textile industry grew rapidly in the Medellín area. Oil drilling began along the Caribbean coast, which was also home to fruit plantations.

The prosperity came to an abrupt end during the worldwide economic depression that began in 1929. This period of economic collapse drastically reduced Colombia's exports and led to poverty, unemployment, and social and political turmoil. While urban workers demanded better wages and working conditions, farmers demanded a more fair distribution of productive land. Voters ousted the Conservative government in 1930, when the Liberal candidate Enrique Olaya Herrera won the presidency.

Liberal control continued with the election of Alfonso López Pumarejo in 1934, and the Liberal Party held power for the next twelve years. The Liberals, who had once favored a weak central government, sought to strengthen federal control over the economy and provincial governments to carry out needed reforms in land ownership, agriculture, trade, and education. New laws and a constitutional reform in 1936 made it possible for the government to seize and redistribute land. But a split within the Liberal Party resulted in the election of the Conservative candidate Mariano Ospina Pérez in 1946. Ospina and other Conservatives still favored a weak central government, a greater role for the Church in public life, and economic policies that benefited business leaders and wealthier landowners.

Unable to resolve their differences, the two factions turned to violence.

THE GREAT BANANA STRIKE

A key event in modern Colombian history is known as the Great Banana Strike. It took place in November 1928 in the Magdalena Department. Workers who picked and packed bananas for the United Fruit Company went on strike. They demanded the right to be employed by the company rather than by labor contractors, who were not required to provide important benefits. The strike turned violent, and the government declared martial law—use of military force to maintain law and order. Dozens of workers were killed by soldiers and police, and the United Fruit Company was targeted with arson and looting.

The Great Banana Strike had important consequences for Colombia. The violence, along with labor problems in other industries, turned many Colombians against the Conservative government.

In 1948 Jorge Eliecer Gaitán, a popular leader in the Liberal Party, was assassinated. His killing sparked a bloody uprising—the bogotazo—in Bogotá. The fighting spread throughout Colombia and lasted for a decade. This period is known as La Violencia, "the Violence." Especially harsh in the countryside, La Violencia caused thousands of rural Colombians to move to cities. The desperately poor families built shantytowns (slums) and struggled to survive.

General Gustavo Rojas Pinilla took power after spearheading a military coup in 1953. After several years of dictatorship, Rojas Pinilla was himself overthrown by the army in 1957. After this event, the Liberal and Conservative parties devised a new political organization, the Frente Nacional (National Front), and a power-sharing agreement. Under the agreement, Liberal and Conservative presidents would alternate every four years. Liberals and Conservatives would also share control of other government and administrative positions. Conservative Guillermo León Valencia served as president from 1962 until 1966, and Liberal Carlos Lleras Restrepo held the office from 1966 until 1970.

Guerrilla Movements

During the 1960s, Colombia further modernized its economy and enjoyed a political truce. But the success of Communist-led revolutions in other regions of Latin America inspired the founding of guerrilla movements in Colombia. Guerrilla groups—independent units engaged in warfare, harassment, and sabotage—fought for political and economic control of the country's rural areas. Inspired by the revolutionary victory in Cuba, the guerrillas aimed to create a Communist state similar to that established by Cuban guerrilla leader Fidel Castro. Colombian guerrilla groups included the Revolutionary Armed Forces of Colombia (abbreviated as FARC, based on the Spanish name), the National Liberation Army (ELN, based on the Spanish name), and the Democratic Alliance. The April 19 Movement, also known as M-19, arose in 1970 in protest of the election of Conservative Misael Pastrana Borrero. While many Colombians protested the Conservatives' handling of the poor economy—which was bringing rising prices and unemployment—the supporters of Pastrana's opponent, General Gustavo Rojas Pinilla, believed that Pastrana's election was fraudulent.

In 1974 the formal power-sharing agreement between the Liberals and the Conservatives came to an end, though a modified version continued. That year the Liberal presidential candidate Alfonso López Michelsen came to power. He was succeeded by a Liberal president, Julio César Turbay Ayala, in 1978 and a Conservative, Belisario Betancur, in 1982. In the meantime, despite the government's efforts to defeat the guerrilla fighting, it raged on in the countryside. President Betancur created the Contadora Group to bring the opposing factions to some sort of agreement. A general cease-fire held until 1985, when guerrillas in the Democratic Alliance and M-19 groups resumed their war. The violence culminated in an assault on the Palace of Justice on November 6, 1985, in which eleven justices of Colombia's Supreme Court were assassinated.

Colombia's struggle with drug trafficking also brought chaos and bloodshed. Drug cartels, or business associations, earned enormous sums of money from the production of cocaine and marijuana. Most of these drugs were exported to the United States. The drug cartels' power undermined the authority of the Colombian government. In the late 1980s, President Virgilio Barco tried to subdue the drug cartels, but the struggle resulted in bombings, assassinations, and kidnappings. During the 1990 elections, three presidential candidates were assassinated by groups associated with drug cartels, the most powerful of which operated out of Medellín.

After the election of Liberal César Gaviria Trujillo in 1990, the Colombian people voted to revise the nation's constitution. The new constitution, which went into effect on July 6, 1991, reformed the

Tanks surround the Palace of Justice in Bogotá in 1985, when guerrillas took hostages inside the building and killed eleven Supreme Court justices. The event was just one of many clashes between government officials and rebel fighters.

judicial system, revamped voting laws, limited the legislature's privileges, and held that presidents could serve only one term.

The Colombian presidency has continued to alternate between parties, though not by formal agreement. Liberal Ernesto Samper Pizano was elected in 1994, and Conservative Andrés Pastrana took office in 1998. Pastrana's efforts to reach a truce with the rebels led to the creation of a large demilitarized zone, a territory that provided a safe haven for the FARC guerrillas. This zone was intended to bring about a truce and renewed peace talks, but negotiations collapsed in February 2002, after FARC rebels kidnapped a prominent politician. The government also accused FARC of using the demilitarized zone for drug running and as a staging ground for attacks against the military and police.

In 2002 Álvaro Uribe Vélez, the former governor of Antioquia, was elected president. Uribe, who did not belong to any political party, promised to crack down on the guerrilla movement and also to rein in the paramilitary death squads that were operating in many areas of the country, sometimes with the cooperation of Colombia's official army. The country's major paramilitary group, the United Self-Defense Forces of Colombia (in Spanish, Autodefensas de Colombia, or AUC), was formed by drug traffickers and landowners to combat guerrilla kidnappings and other acts. The AUC is considered among the most brutal forces in the conflict.

Although some leaders of the guerrilla movements, including M-19, have entered the political mainstream, fighting between the guerrillas and paramilitary groups continues to challenge the government. The violence has touched the highest levels of Colombian society, including prominent political leaders such as presidential candidate Ingrid Betancourt, who was kidnapped along with her campaign manager, Clara Rojas, in February 2002. Drug trafficking also brings violence, corruption, and a host of other social problems.

Colombian president **Álvaro Uribe Vélez** has worked to curb guerrilla violence in his nation. Find reports on current events in Colombia at vgsbooks.com.

Some of Uribe's early efforts to deal with violence and the drug trade met with approval, but he was criticized for enlisting more financial and military aid from the United States. In August 2002, Uribe declared that Colombia had entered a state of unrest, and he called on Colombian civilians to join a national militia force to help combat the government's opponents.

In an effort to convince the rebels to lay down their arms, President Uribe's government offered amnesty, or pardon—including a temporary salary and job training—to guerrilla fighters in 2003. Although some guerrillas surrendered to accept the offer, bombings, assassinations, and kidnappings have continued in many regions, making it all but impossible for the local population to carry out business and normal daily life.

The conflict also has affected relations between Colombia and its neighbor to the east, Venezuela. In early 2003, Colombia accused the government of Venezuela of allowing rebel leaders to hide in Venezuelan territory near the border between the two nations. The issue of rebel sanctuaries within Venezuela continued to damage relations between Venezuela and Colombia through early 2003.

⊙ Government

Colombia is governed under a constitution that was passed in 1886 and broadly amended in 1991. The federal government is divided into three branches—executive, legislative, and judicial. All Colombian citizens over age eighteen can vote to elect a president every four years. If no candidate receives more than 50 percent of the vote, a second election is held between the two leading vote winners. The president, who can serve just one term, appoints ministers. In the past, Colombia didn't have a vice president, but the 1991 constitution created the position. As in the United States, a candidate for president chooses a vice presidential running mate.

The Colombian legislature is made up of two houses, a 102-member Senate and a 165-member House of Representatives. The country holds legislative elections every four years.

The highest court in Colombia is known as the Corte Suprema de Justicia, or Supreme Court of Justice. Twenty-four Supreme Court judges serve eight-year terms. The Council of State is the highest court for administrative matters, while the Constitutional Court rules on the constitutionality of new laws, international treaties, and proposed amendments to the Constitution. A fourth high court, the Higher Council of Justice, deals with the judicial system itself. There are also criminal, civil, and labor courts, as well as county and appellate courts in the departments.

Colombia is divided into thirty-two departments and a federal capital district. Each department has a governor and a legislature. Colombian cities and towns are headed by mayors.

THE PEOPLE

Historians have labeled Colombia the "most Spanish" of the South American countries. Colombia's history is tied to Spain, and Colombian art and writing have been influenced by Spanish works and ideas. Much of Colombia's European population originally came from Spain. The Roman Catholic Church still dominates religious life in Colombia, and the official language remains Castilian Spanish, the language of the conquistadors. Colombians have created their own unique society, however.

A Mixed, Growing Population

During the colonial period, many European settlers married indigenous people. As a result, a majority of Colombians are mestizos. Mestizos make up about half of the population. Another 15 to 25 percent are mulato, or of mixed European and African heritage. Whites make up about 20 percent of the population, while blacks make up about 5 percent.

Approximately 1 percent of Colombians trace their heritage to indigenous peoples. Some of the major indigenous groups include the Aymará, Arawak, Chibcha, Carib, Quechua, Tupi-Guarani, and Yurumangui. Most of these native peoples live in isolated rural regions where modern civilization has made few inroads. The Guajiro, for example, live in the arid and undeveloped Guajira Peninsula. In such places, the people have little contact with the outside world, and they may have developed and kept their own distinctive clothing, speech, and customs.

Even in the largest cities of Colombia, however, people also have their particular customs and society. The Bogotanos (people of Bogotá), for example, see themselves as distinct from the people who live in Medellín or Cali. An important social group is the Antioqueños, or people from the Antioquia Department, who dominate Colombian industry and finance, as well as the coffee business.

Colombia's population density varies widely, but more than nine out of ten Colombians live in the western half of the country, along

These Kogi girls live in the Sierra Nevada de Santa Marta. The Kogi refer to the mountain range they inhabit as the "heart of the world."

KOGI INDEPENDENCE

The Kogi people, who live in the Sierra Nevada de Santa Marta, have held on to their cultural and religious traditions in defiance of industrialization, population growth, and development. Descendants of the Tayrona people, the Kogi fled into the Santa Marta range to escape colonization and enslavement by the Spanish. Since then the Kogi have remained very protective of their land and culture. Their remote villages are closed to the outside world, including tourists and ordinary Colombians.

the Caribbean coast, in the valleys dividing the Andean ranges, and in a few cities on the Pacific coast. The population clusters in and around the major cities—Bogotá, Medellín, and Cali—and in the Magdalena and Cauca river valleys. Many rural Colombians have left their farms and villages to settle in these cities. The cities' newest residents often suffer poverty, unemployment, and poor living conditions. About 71 percent of the Colombian population is urban, slightly less than the average of 79 percent for South America as a whole. About one-third of Colombians live in the nation's six largest cities, while the large but sparsely populated regions of the Llanos and the Amazonian forests of the southeast are home to only about 2 percent of the population.

Colombia's population grew rapidly in the 1990s and early 2000s. With a total population of 43.8 million, Colombia is the most populous Spanish-speaking nation of South America, well ahead of second-place Argentina. (Brazil, where Portuguese is the main language, is the most populous country in South

America.) Colombia's rapid population growth has been balanced to some extent by the emigration of skilled workers seeking better opportunities outside the country.

Education

Despite Colombia's social and political turmoil, the country has achieved a high literacy rate—more than 90 percent in urban areas. Children between the ages of six and twelve are legally required to attend primary school. But many young people, especially those working on farms, attend only a few years of school or none at all. Students must complete five years of primary school to go on to secondary school. While about 90 percent of all Colombian children attend primary school, only about 50 percent enroll in secondary school.

After four years of secondary school, students can choose to pursue job training or continue their education. Before graduating, students must take the Bachiller examination, a ritual dreaded by every Colombian high school student. Colombia has twenty-five public universities, the most prestigious of which is the National University of Colombia in Bogotá.

About 40 percent of all students in Colombia attend private schools, many of which are run by the Catholic Church. Some private

A group of students from a Catholic private school chat between classes.

schools teach in English as well as Spanish. Many families choose private schools because public schools are often overcrowded, and in some areas, nearly half of all public school students do not graduate. The private schools are credited with helping raise the country's literacy rate and for preparing more students for university study. Attendance at Colombian universities has risen from about 10,000 in the early 1970s to more than 500,000 in the early twenty-first century.

Health and Welfare

During the 1980s, the health care system in Colombia changed dramatically. The central government surrendered much of its control over public health to the departments and municipalities. Colombian mayors, who serve as heads of local health systems, must adopt a comprehensive health plan to combat disease epidemics, poor sanitation, and other health issues. The federal Ministry of Labor and Social Security certifies local health organizations, a process meant to assure higher standards for hospitals, clinics, and doctor training. The results of this decentralization have been uneven. While many areas have benefited from local control, in other places health services are still lacking. Rural areas do not have enough trained nurses and doctors. Although Colombia requires all doctors to work for at least a year in the countryside as part of their training, the majority of these physicians eventually move to the cities.

In an effort to wipe out the drug trade, Colombia sprays many areas of the country with herbicides. These chemicals are designed to kill the coca plant, which is the raw material for the illegal drug cocaine. But the spraying is killing and injuring people as well as plants. In the department of Putumayo, several people have died from breathing glyphosate, a herbicide that is sprayed over fields near villages. The fumes also cause headaches, sore eyes, gastrointestinal problems, and skin irritation.

Overall, Colombia has managed to improve its public health. The country's infant mortality rate, at 21 deaths per 1,000 births, remains lower than the average for South America, which is 29 deaths per 1,000 births. Life expectancy in Colombia is 71 years (68 for males and 74 for females), which is about average in South America.

Colombians still suffer from a variety of local diseases, including malaria, dysentery, typhoid, and cholera. Unhealthy urban slums provide a fertile breeding ground for infectious diseases. Malnutrition affects people in rural areas, where communications are poor and many laborers do not earn enough money to keep food on the table.

The immune system disease AIDS has also struck Colombia, although at a lower rate than elsewhere in South America. In 1999 approximately 70,000 Colombians were carrying the AIDS virus. Most of these people live in large cities. The AIDS rate is higher along the Caribbean coast, where the population mixes most freely with tourists and other outsiders. The rate is lower in more isolated highland regions and in the Llanos.

The Colombian government runs a social security system that provides benefits for disabled, elderly, and unemployed people, injured and sick workers, and women on maternity leave. In addition, a public pension system provides benefits for retired workers.

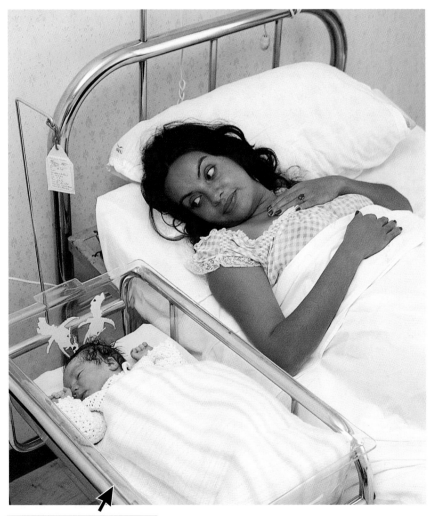

Women on maternity leave are among the groups that receive benefits from Colombia's national social security system, *el Instituto de Seguros Sociales.*

To find out more about the various customs of people in Colombia, including various indigenous groups, learn some basic Spanish words, and get the most up-to-date population figures, visit vgsbooks.com.

Religion

The vast majority of Colombians belong to the Roman Catholic Church, which played an important role in the settlement of Latin America. The Catholic Church still runs many private schools and universities in Colombia, though it must follow educational guidelines established by the government. Religious welfare programs benefit the poor and the unemployed, and Catholic clergy remain influential with many people, especially in rural areas, where village priests are respected community leaders.

In 1973 the Colombian government and the Vatican—the Roman Catholic leadership—signed an agreement that ended Catholicism's status as the official national religion of Colombia. The agreement, called a Concordat, also recognized the Church as the religion of the

A children's choir gathers in front of their Catholic church. Catholicism was once the official national religion of Colombia.

great majority of Colombians. The Concordat allowed for civil marriages (those held outside of the Church). The Concordat also ended the Church's authority over public schools and public services for indigenous peoples, and it banned Catholic censorship of public school textbooks. Although some Catholic schools use separate books, published by Catholic publishers, these books must conform to standards established by the federal government.

The Colombian constitution guarantees freedom of worship. A small Protestant community, numbering about 200,000, remains active in Colombia, even though Protestant missionaries have met strong resistance from the Catholic Church. The San Andrés y Providencia island chain is home to a community of black Protestants, who accepted this faith when the islands were originally colonized by the British. Jewish enclaves have survived in some of Colombia's large cities.

A SMALL, DIVERSE COMMUNITY

Colombia's Jewish community of about six thousand people dates back to the 1600s, a time when many Jews came to Latin America to escape persecution in Europe. In Colombia, Jewish families cleared farming estates, built towns and businesses, and, in 1616, founded the city of Medellín. Modern Medellín, Cali, Barranquilla, and Bogotá all have Jewish communities. Jewish people in Bogotá may attend Conservative, Orthodox, or Sephardic synagogues. The capital city also has a Hebrew day school, as well as Jewish publications and radio shows.

Traces of African religions survive among the descendants of slaves who lived along the Caribbean coast. A few indigenous tribes continue to practice traditional religions as well, although most of Colombia's native peoples were converted by Catholic missionaries.

CULTURAL LIFE

Colombians have developed a lively scene in art, music, and literature. Many of the nation's most important artists live and work in the capital, Bogotá, which has become a cultural mecca. The Bogotanos carry on a strong rivalry with the city of Medellín, where people can visit dozens of art galleries and art exhibitions. Writers in Colombia enjoy a freedom of expression unknown in many other parts of Latin America, and the Colombian news media operates without government censorship.

Traditionally, Colombian culture was linked closely to that of Spain. Spanish art and architecture influenced Colombia's buildings, and Spanish literary styles dominated Colombian writing during the 1700s and 1800s. But in the twentieth century, Colombia broke away from its European ties and developed several distinct artistic traditions of its own.

◉ Art and Architecture

Colombia has a rich artistic heritage, beginning with important works created long before the arrival of the Europeans. Around 500 B.C., the inhabitants of San Agustín created monumental stone sculptures of their gods and animal spirits. The people of San Agustín also developed several different styles of pottery. Many indigenous groups used gold and other metals to decorate their faces and bodies. The Tolima and Quimbaya people created stunning gold figurines and pectorals, or protective chest armor worn by soldiers.

The Spaniards who settled in Colombia brought European paintings and sculptures to their new country. These works influenced generations of Colombian artists. The colonists also created religious art in many forms—paintings, statues, and altarpieces. During the colonial era, several painted images, including the *Virgin of Monguí* and the *Virgin of Chiquinquirá*, became the focus of popular cults. Believers credited the paintings with miraculous powers.

The best-known colonial artist, Gregorio Vásquez de Arce y Ceballos, lived in the 1600s. Other important artists of the time include Angelino Medoro, Francisco de Páramo, and Pedro Bedón, a friar (a Christian monk) who worked in Tunja, a religious and artistic center. The Baroque style of religious architecture, imported from Spain, dominated the cities of colonial Colombia. This architectural style is known for its elaborate decoration and sculpture. Colonial churches and monasteries still stand in Colombia, and an entire colonial city has survived in the old quarter of modern Cartagena. The old town is protected by an impressive wall built in the 1700s to ward off pirates.

Modern European art influenced Colombia's twentieth-century artists, including Pedro Nel Gómez, a muralist, and painters Luis Alberto Acuña and Alejandro Obregón. One of Colombia's best-known artists is Fernando Botero. His satirical artwork depicts outsize human figures. Armando Villegas is known for his surrealistic paintings that draw on pre-Columbian themes. Rodrigo Arenas Betancourt was the country's leading twentieth-century sculptor. His fanciful statues are a prominent feature of Colombia's urban landscape.

Some of the most skilled Colombian artists work in crafts. Goldsmithing and jewelry making remain respected arts, and many ancient indigenous techniques are still used. Weavers fashion brightly colored clothing and blankets from cotton and wool. Basket weaving employs the majority of adults in many small towns and villages, including Sandona. Weavers from Sandona invented the palm-fiber Panama hat, which was first made for workers digging the Panama Canal early in the twentieth century.

A Guajiro woman weaves a hammock. Handmade weavings are prized as craft items.

A potter displays his wares in front of his Boyacá shop. **Earthenware ceramics** have been an important part of Colombian culture for centuries.

In Ráquira, in the Boyacá Department, potters copy the forms and decorations used by the Chibcha people. Craft workers in the town of Pasto use a seed resin called barniz, which they hammer into thin sheets, dye in various colors, cut, then glue over wooden masks and other objects.

Music

Colombia's musical traditions combine native forms and rhythms with those brought by the Spanish conquerors. Indigenous people of Colombia fashioned a variety of flutes and drums and performed music during ceremonies and festivals.

Spanish settlers introduced European instruments to Colombia, while African slaves brought their musical traditions as well. The African-based music of the Caribbean basin has been an important influence on Colombian music. In the early 1900s, lively folk songs called *vallenatos* provided not only entertainment but also a way of spreading news and gossip from one place to the next. African and Latin influences show up in modern

Folk musician

Parade participants **dance the cumbia** during an annual agricultural fair.

dance rhythms such as salsa, *cumbia,* and merengue. Colombians also enjoy music from Cuba and Mexico, as well as the tango, a sultry dance that was invented in Argentina.

The music of the Andes Mountains differs from that along the coasts. Stringed instruments are popular in highland villages, where popular musical forms include the *bambuco,* a dance form that grew out of solo voice serenades, and the *pasillo,* a waltz that is also popular in Ecuador and Venezuela. Another important Colombian musical style is *música llanera,* or music of the Llanos, which is played with a harp, guitar, and the bean-filled gourds known as the maracas.

Colombia's best-known composer in the classical tradition, Guillermo Uribe-Holguín, produced more than five hundred works, including symphonies, string quartets, trios, concerti, sonatas, and songs. After studying in Europe from 1907 to 1910, Uribe-Holguín returned to his native city of Bogotá, where he helped to establish the National Conservatory and the National Symphony in 1910.

Literature

Colombians pride themselves on a long and acclaimed literary tradition. Important novels and works of poetry were composed during the colonial era, and nineteenth-century authors made political statements through their works. José Eustacio Rivera's 1924 novel, *La*

Vorágine (The Vortex), describes a man's journey through the Colombian countryside and his experience of the violent conflict over the valuable rubber trees of the rain forest.

During the 1950s, the literary journal *Mito* became the center of a thriving national literature. During this time, author Gabriel García Márquez came to prominence with novels set in a mythical place known as Macondo. In 1982 García Márquez was awarded the Nobel Prize in Literature. This honor established Colombia's place on the world's literary scene and remains a point of national pride.

García Márquez's works, which also include short stories and film scripts, challenge the social and political norms of his country. His most famous book is *One Hundred Years of Solitude,* published in 1967. This work was widely translated and became an international best-seller, as did two later novels, *The Autumn of the Patriarch* (1976) and *Love in the Time of Cholera* (1988).

Another well-known writer from García Márquez's generation is Álvaro Mutis, a poet and novelist. Younger writers include Gustavo Álvarez Gardeazabal, Albalucia Ángel, and Fanny Buitrago. The essay is a vital form of modern Colombian writing, popularized by Germán Arciniegas and Otto Morales Benítez. Juan Gustavo Cobo Borda publishes poems, essays, and literary criticism.

Nobel Prize winner **Gabriel García Márquez** is credited with creating a style of writing called magical realism.

Fernando Vallejo, a novelist and film director, wrote *La Virgen de los Sicarios (Our Lady of the Assassins),* an account of the cocaine trade and the havoc it brought to the city of Medellín. Published in 1994, the novel paints a detailed portrait of a society suffering from greed, self-interest, and relentless violence. Vallejo's films include *Barrio de Campeones (District of Champions),* produced in 1985, which describes the harsh choices confronting a single mother in modern Colombia.

Sports

Like many other South American nations, Colombia has an avid following for soccer. Professional teams attract huge crowds to their matches, and millions also take part in amateur and youth leagues. Carlos Valderrama, a Colombian soccer legend, played for teams in South America, France, and the United States.

Colombians also enjoy a wide variety of other spectator sports. Automobile racing is probably the country's fastest-growing spectator

Two soccer teams face off in a Cali stadium. Soccer is a national passion in Colombia, as it is in other parts of Latin America.

sport. Basketball teams compete in the big cities, and baseball has found an audience, especially among younger Colombians along the Caribbean coast. Competitions in biking, tennis, and boxing also draw fans. Large crowds in many cities and towns still attend traditional bull-fights, a sport brought from Spain.

Popular recreational activities include hiking and mountain climbing in the Andes highlands and scuba diving along the Caribbean coast. Colombia has a national organization dedicated to mountain biking and has produced a world-champion mountain biker, Santiago Botero.

At the 2000 Olympic Games in Sydney, Australia, weight lifter María Isabel Urrutia became the first Colombian in history to win an Olympic gold medal. Before the games, Urrutia had to lose 45 pounds (20 kg) in order to compete in her 165-pound (75-kg) weight class.

Holidays

Colombians celebrate many holidays throughout the year, including several Christian festivals and observances. Carnaval, or Carnival, heralds the coming of the Easter season. Carnaval, called Mardi Gras in some countries, is a time for having fun before the more somber period of Lent, the forty days preceding Easter. During Lent many Catholics give up certain foods. The city of Barranquilla is famous for its lively Carnaval, which attracts celebrants from all over Colombia for parades, music, and dancing in the streets. The Easter holidays include Palm Sunday, Maundy Thursday, Good Friday, and Ascension,

Men in the town of Buga carry a float in an Easter parade. Easter and other Christian holidays play an important role in Colombian culture.

which marks the day that, according to Christian tradition, Christ rose to heaven. The Feast of St. Peter and Paul, which celebrates two founders of the Church, takes place on June 29, while August 15 is Assumption, which marks the rising or "assumption" of the Virgin Mary into heaven. On November 1, Colombian families pay respect to the dead and to the saints on All Saints' Day.

The Christmas season begins on December 7, when Colombian Christians light candles in honor of the Virgin Mary. The following day is the Immaculate Conception, a national holiday. Many families set up Christmas trees and nativity scenes in their homes, and on midnight on Christmas Eve, friends and families exchange gifts.

Among the civic holidays are Labor Day, on May 1, and Independence Day, July 20. A second independence day, on November 11, celebrates the independence of Cartagena, the first city to declare freedom from Spanish rule. The people of Cartagena celebrate with parades, street fairs, and the National Beauty Contest, in which Miss Colombia is selected. Parades take place throughout the country on

Military parades are common in Independence Day celebrations in Colombia.

August 7, when Colombians pay tribute to the Battle of Boyacá, in which Simón Bolívar defeated the Spanish army and won independence for Colombia.

The celebration of the European discovery of the Americas takes place on October 12, Columbus Day. Like many civic and religious holidays, Columbus Day moves to the following Monday when October 12 does not fall on a Monday. Colombians then can enjoy the *puente,* a three-day weekend that includes a public holiday.

Go to vgsbooks.com. Click on the various cultural links to websites where you'll find recipes, photos of holidays and festivals in Colombia, and more.

◉ Food

Like people in many Latin American societies, Colombians break in the middle of the day for a noontime meal, called *almuerzo.* The *comida,* or evening meal, can begin as early as 6 P.M. but often takes place later. Many meals in Colombia begin with soup. *Ajiaco* is a soup from Bogotá made with chicken, potatoes, and corn, accompanied by avocado. *Sancocho* is another favorite soup that contains vegetables with fish, meat, or chicken.

Soup may be followed by a main course of meat, chicken, or fish, served with vegetables and rice, beans, lentils, or pasta. Fried plantains

Colombian meals often include rich ingredients such as avocados, plantains, and rice.

Hormigas culonas are not a snack for the squeamish! These specially raised ants have an enlarged abdomen, which is the only part of them that is eaten. Hormigas culonas are often served with a wedge of cheese or a small container of honey.

BIG BUTT ANTS

A crunchy specialty of the Colombian department of Santander is *hormigas culonas*, or "big butt ants." Fried in oil and salted, the ants are a popular street food. Those who like hormigas culonas say they taste like peanuts.

and salads also are popular side dishes. Throughout the cities of Colombia, food stalls provide freshly cooked meals to busy workers who can't take the time to go home for their midday meal.

Among the most popular dishes in Colombia is *carne asada,* or roasted meat served with rice, chips, or plantains. *Arroz con pollo* is chicken with rice, vegetables, and potatoes or chips. *Bandeja paisa*, a dish that is popular in Antioquia, includes red beans, minced beef, sausage, rice, plantains, a corn pancake, and avocado. A popular street food is *fritanga,* simply a dish of fried meat, which may be sausage, pork rinds, or a variety of organ meats, served with corn on the cob, plantains, or potatoes. In San Andrés y Providencia, many cooks prepare *rondón,* a dish of coconut milk, cassava, plantains, fish, and snails.

To accompany a meal, Colombians drink fruit juice, bottled water, or coffee. A leader in coffee production, Colombia has created several

A family gathers for the evening meal near their stall in an open-air market. Colombians enjoy socializing with family and friends over a meal.

varieties of this beverage. Coffee drinkers can choose *tinto* (a small, strong cup of coffee), *café con leche* (coffee with milk added), or *pintado* (half milk, half coffee). The traditional coffee recipe calls for a tablespoon of ground beans and a spoonful of sugar for each cup. Colombians also drink *aromáticas* (herbal teas) and *gaseosas* (carbonated soft drinks).

NATILLA

This sweet custard, made with cornstarch, is popular throughout Latin America. Many cooks also add raisins to the *natilla*.

1½ cups cornstarch

4 cups milk

1½ cups brown sugar

4 or 5 cinnamon sticks, or 1 tablespoon ground cinnamon

1 cup shredded coconut

1. Dissolve the cornstarch in the milk. Add the brown sugar. Cook over low heat, stirring constantly.
2. When the sugar is melted and the custard begins to thicken, add the cinnamon and coconut. Stir well.
3. When custard is very thick, remove cinnamon sticks, if used. Pour custard into a large serving dish. Cover and refrigerate for 2 hours or overnight. Serve cold, in small bowls.

Serves 4

THE ECONOMY

Despite political upheaval and violence, Colombia enjoyed a fast-growing economy in the early twenty-first century. While many other Latin American nations experienced crippling foreign debts and steeply rising prices, Colombia managed to escape these economic ills. Unlike many of its neighbors, Colombia repaid loans made by foreign banks and countries. The Colombian government encouraged business development by allowing private industries to borrow public funds and by lowering taxes for new businesses. Between 1950 and 2000, the economy grew an average of 4.2 percent a year—the fastest growth rate in South America.

Colombia's government launched a sweeping economic reform program in the early 1990s, lifting many restrictions on foreign trade and cutting public spending. At the same time, the discovery of new oil reserves in the sector of the Casanare department that falls in the Llanos plains boosted economic production. By the mid-1990s, however, the economy began to slow down. Unemployment rose, prices for coffee and

oil fell, and Colombia saw a decline in gross domestic product (GDP)—
the total amount of goods and services produced within a country's borders. Guerrilla groups made matters worse by sabotaging electrical power
installations and oil drilling, refining, and pipeline facilities.

Although a severe recession hit Colombia in 1999, causing a drop
in economic activity, the country quickly recovered, and GDP rose by
3 percent in 2000. Colombia allowed its currency, the peso, to "float"
on the world markets. This policy meant that instead of being held to
a fixed exchange rate, the value of the peso could rise and fall with
supply and demand, making it more affordable for foreigners to invest
in Colombian industry.

Over the past few decades, industry has gradually replaced agriculture as the mainstay of the economy, and a prosperous middle class
has emerged. But the prosperity has been divided unequally among
Colombia's people. Low wages and high unemployment still affected
rural families and a large segment of urban workers, many of whom

were first- or second-generation migrants from isolated, mountainous, or rural regions. By some estimates, the richest 10 percent of Colombians hold 44 percent of the country's wealth, while the poorest 10 percent hold just 1 percent. Despite the growing economy, millions of poor citizens still live in huge slums on the outskirts of cities.

Colombia is also home to a huge underground economy—trade in illegal drugs and other goods that bypasses the normal channels of sales, distribution, and taxation. Precious gemstones such as emeralds and exotic wildlife such as macaws and other rain forest birds are sold on the black market. Crime and corruption brought by these underground activities have been disrupting Colombian society for many years, and political leaders still grapple with the problems associated with the drug trade.

Macaw

◎ Services

Colombia's emerging service economy has come to dominate the economic life of the country's largest cities. Banking is a vital sector of the service economy, providing credit for private companies and a channel for transactions with foreign nations and business firms. By some estimates, banking, insurance, and other financial businesses contribute 15 percent to Colombia's gross domestic product.

Employees at the Bank of the Republic in Bogotá check freshly printed notes for defects. Banking is one of the largest industries in Colombia.

The retail sector, along with hotels and restaurants, runs a close second among service industries. Transportation companies, including Colombia's national airline, Avianca, provide service to tourists as well as Colombians. Flights link Colombian cities large and small, offering a practical alternative to the poor road and railroad networks.

◎ Agriculture and Forestry

Although only about 5 percent of the land in Colombia is suitable for farming, agriculture makes up about 19 percent of GDP. Agricultural businesses employ nearly four million Colombians—about 30 percent of the workforce. Coffee has been an important agricultural product in Colombia since the early 1800s, when the first commercial coffee plantations were established. In modern times, Colombia is second only to Brazil in the production and export of coffee beans. The small departments of Caldas, Risaralda, and Quindío in west-central Colombia make up the "coffee zone," where coffee cultivation dominates the local economy.

With a variety of soils and climates, Colombia produces a range of useful agricultural products, including cotton, cacao, tobacco, corn, rice, wheat, barley, potatoes, and beans. The traditional food staple of Colombia, maize (corn), grows throughout the country.

A coffee picker harvests beans for drying and processing. Although subject to rising and falling market prices, coffee remains a staple product of the Colombian economy.

Workers use a horse to help load **just-harvested sugarcane** onto a truck at the edge of a field near Buga, in the Cauca River Valley.

Large sugarcane plantations flourish in the Cauca River Valley. Bananas and plantains, grown along the Caribbean coast, are the nation's most important fruit crops.

Livestock, particularly beef cattle, are important both as a source of meat and for hides, which are exported to make leather products. Fishing in the Amazonian rivers provides a food source for people in eastern Colombia, but ocean fishing has not been developed as a commercial industry. The Colombian forestry industry still ranks well behind that of neighboring countries, as the heavily forested regions near the Amazon River remain difficult to access.

◉ Manufacturing

Colombian industries have benefited from favorable government policies, extensive foreign investment, and a well-developed hydroelectric power industry, which supplies factories with inexpensive energy. The government has set up the Institute of Industrial Development to foster new businesses, such as automobile manufacturing, steel manufacturing, and metalworking, that require large amounts of initial capital (start-up money). In 2000 manufacturing employed about two million Colombian workers, or a little more than 10 percent of the total workforce.

Colombian factories produce automobiles, paper, petroleum products, and household goods such as appliances and furniture. The textile industry, centered in Medellín, is the country's largest employer, making finished clothing and fabric for sale to domestic and international markets. Colombia's chemical industry provides dyes and processing chemicals to textile makers. In the early 1950s, Colombia built its first steel plant at

Panama hats *(on bottom, with black bands)* and other woven hats are practical in sunny countries near the equator.

Paz del Río in the Boyacá Department, and this plant still meets most of the nation's demand for steel.

Mining and Energy

During the colonial era, gold was key to Colombia's wealth. Early settlers mined gold from the ground or stole it from indigenous tribes. Gold remains an important resource into the twenty-first century, with more than six hundred gold mines operating in the Antioquia Department. Gold mining also takes place in the Chocó Department.

Colombia's other mineral resources include valuable metals and precious gems. Mines in the Cordillera Oriental produce copper, nickel, limestone, and marble. South America's only platinum deposits are found in Colombia, in the Chocó Department. Colombia is also the world's leading producer of emeralds, which are mined from riverbeds and hillsides in the Cordillera Oriental. The precious stones are sold in public markets in Bogotá and other Colombian cities, drawing buyers from all over the world.

A pair of gold miners in the Santander Department prepare to sort through a pile of minerals in search of the precious metal.

Coal mines such as El Cerrejon, near the Guajira Peninsula, provide energy for Colombia and other countries.

Colombia began exploiting its energy resources of coal and oil in the mid-1900s. Colombia has the largest deposits of coal in South America, in the Andes mountains as well as the northern department of La Guajira. The Caño Limón pipeline in Arauca provides crude oil, supplemented by drilling in Casanare, where a large oil field was discovered in the 1990s and is believed to be one of the biggest in the world. New pipelines carry the crude oil to terminals on the Pacific Ocean.

Colombia's many fast-flowing rivers provide significant hydropower potential. But hydroelectric production has been hampered by poor security in the countryside and a severe drought in the early 1990s. Colombia is also developing thermal energy plants, which use coal and natural gas as fuel sources.

◉ Foreign Trade

Colombia's economy has been bolstered by exports. For years the nation has kept a healthy balance of trade—meaning it exports more than it imports—and has provided manufactured as well as agricultural goods to foreign buyers. The major exports include coal, textiles, petroleum, cotton, cacao, coffee, bananas, and sugar. Colombian

Workers at a Bogotá flower exporter prepare **carnations and roses** for shipping.

A FLOWERING BUSINESS

Colombia has become the number two producer of fresh-cut flowers in the world, after the Netherlands. Greenhouses and flower beds dot the landscape around Bogotá, where growers benefit from being close to Bogotá's international airport. After cutting the flowers, growers rush them to waiting cargo planes. The blooms are flown to markets across Latin America and North America. The United States buys about 75 percent of the exported flowers.

flower growers, concentrated in the Bogotá region, export a wide variety of fresh-cut flowers all over the world.

Coffee alone accounted for about half of all export earnings through the 1970s, and Colombia still ranks second only to Brazil in the amount of coffee exported. This has made the national economy vulnerable to swings in the price of coffee. Colombians responded to this weakness by diversifying the export trade. By the twenty-first century, coffee made up less than one-third of all export earnings. Energy products such as petroleum and coal have replaced coffee as the leading exports. Petroleum production, however, has declined, and oil drillers are hard pressed to replace drying wells with oil from newly discovered fields.

Colombia imports machinery, chemicals, paper, metal products, transportation equipment, and refined petroleum products such as aviation fuel and gasoline. Agricultural imports have been declining since the mid-1900s, when Colombia's farming estates were modernized and became more efficient.

Colombia's single most important trading partner is the United States, but the country also trades goods and services with members of the European Union (EU). About 20 percent of foreign trade remains takes place within South America and the Caribbean countries.

Visit vgsbooks.com for up-to-date information about Colombia's economy and a converter with the current exchange rate where you can learn how many pesos are in one U.S. dollar.

The Future

Colombia has avoided many of the economic problems, such as staggering debts, that plague other countries in Latin America. Many deep-seated problems remain, however, including high unemployment, widespread poverty, income disparities, civil conflict, government corruption, illegal drug production, and a guerrilla war that has lasted more than four decades. This ongoing warfare has placed many regions of the country out of reach of government control. The conflict also discourages foreign investors, who worry about the security of their investments in an unstable country.

Many Colombian voters feel apathetic about their elected leaders' ability to solve the country's political and social problems. Government corruption fuels popular support for the guerrilla movement, which remains strong. Colombia faces the challenge of overcoming both the doubts of its own citizens and the fears of foreign investors who could help the economy grow and bring new prosperity.

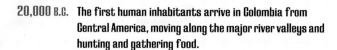

Timeline

20,000 B.C. The first human inhabitants arrive in Colombia from Central America, moving along the major river valleys and hunting and gathering food.

CA. 500 B.C. Indigenous people of San Agustín create massive stone sculptures and pottery.

CA. A.D. 700 Tayrona people build a large, terraced village that is later known as La Ciudad Perdida.

1501 The Spanish explorers Rodrigo de Bastidas and Juan de la Cosa explore the Caribbean coast of Colombia.

1525 Santa Marta, the first Spanish settlement in Colombia, is established.

1536 Sebastián de Belalcázar, part of the South American expedition led by Francisco Pizarro, invades Colombia from the south.

1538 Gonzalo Jiménez de Quesada founds the city of Santafé de Bogotá.

1549 Jiménez de Quesada establishes the Audiencia of New Granada, a division of the Viceroyalty of Peru, in Bogotá.

1717 The Spanish crown establishes the Viceroyalty of New Granada, which includes present-day Colombia, Panama, Venezuela, and Ecuador.

1766 Naturalist José Celestino Mutis begins research on the medicinal properties of quinine.

1777 Colombia's first public library opens in Bogotá.

1794 Journalist Antonio Nariño translates a French revolutionary document, *Declaration of the Rights of Man and of the Citizen*, into Spanish. The manifesto helps spur the independence movement in the Viceroyalty of New Granada.

1811 The city of Cartagena becomes the first in the viceroyalty to declare its independence from Spain. Several other cities form independent provincial governments.

1815 The Spanish reconquer the Viceroyalty of New Granada, harshly repressing the independence movement.

1819 Simón Bolívar defeats the Spanish at the Battle of Boyacá, leading to the creation of Gran Colombia, which includes Colombia, Panama, Ecuador, Venezuela, and parts of Bolivia and northern Peru. Bolívar is president of the new country.

1826 The National Academy is founded to foster scientific research, education, and literature.

1830 Venezuela and Ecuador secede from Gran Colombia, and Gran Colombia is renamed the Republic of New Granada.

ANTONIO NARIÑO (1765–1823) Born in Bogotá, Nariño was a journalist who favored total independence from Spain. He published a Spanish translation of Thomas Paine's *The Rights of Man* (an important document of the American Revolution) in 1793. Nariño was twice taken prisoner by the Spanish and became a legislator after Colombia became independent.

MANUEL ELKIN PATARROYO (b. 1947) Patarroyo is a doctor who helped to develop one of the first vaccines against malaria. He was born in Ataco, in the Tolima Department, and studied at the National University of Bogotá. He later founded the Immunology Institute in the Colombian capital.

RAFAEL REYES (1850–1921) Born in Sant. Rosa while Colombia was still called New Granada, Reyes was elect ᵈ president of Colombia in 1904. He played a key role in reun ʲving tʰ ountry after the War of a Thousand Days and established ᵖ ᵉctiᵛ ·ade barriers to benefit Colombian industries. He also cᵣ ˡ aᵈ tional Assembly, with three representatives from each tᵉ ᵗ ·, to replace the old Colombian legislature, known as tʰ

FRANCISCO DE PAULA SANTANDER charismatic miliᵗ tary officer, Santander was acting ᵖ n Colombia from 1821 to 1827 and president of New ᵗ ²33 to 1837. He helped to organize Colombia's admᵢ ˡ, and public education systems. He was born in ᴮ

SHAKIRA (b. 1977) A pop singer anᵈ ·ranquilla, Shakira signed her first record deal at ˡ ᵗ her first album in 1991, when she was fourte ˡ fame with her third record, *¿Dónde estáɾ ᵈ ᵗ the Thieves?).* Shakira has an internatiᵒ ᶠᵒ in English as well as Spanish and was ɾ ₙina ʸ award in 2003 for her song "Te Aviso Te Aᵢ Told You).

CARLOS VALDERRAMA (b. 1961) A soccᵉ star Marta, Valderrama began his careᵉ wi Magdalena team. He joined the World Cᵘ p squ played for the Tampa Bay Mutiny of ᵗᵉ U Valderrama was named South Americanᵖ ayeɾ

For a link where you caᵣ
"Himno Nacional," go tᵒ

Sights to See

CATEDRAL DE SAL (CATHEDRAL OF SALT) This huge underground cathedral in Zipaquirá, near Bogotá, was built by miners in the 1950s and redesigned in the 1990s. The cathedral can hold almost one thousand worshippers and contains statues, altars, columns, and passageways carved entirely from salt.

CERRO DE MONSERRATE This white church built on the summit of a mountain dominates the Bogotá skyline. Visitors enjoy a breathtaking, panoramic view of the city. They can reach the top by cable car or by funicular, a cable railway that climbs the mountain.

LA CIUDAD PERDIDA This "lost city" of the Tayrona people was built in about A.D. 700 in the Sierra Nevada de Santa Marta highlands. The remains of the site were discovered in 1975 by archaeologist Julio César Sepúlveda. The village was built as a series of several hundred terraces, connected to each other with stone steps and passages.

LAGUNA DE GUATAVITA (LAKE GUATAVITA) This sacred lake of the Muisca Indians gave birth to the myth of El Dorado—the legendary land of riches sought by the Spanish conquistadors. Over the centuries, the lake was drained several times in the search for gold, emeralds, and other treasures. In 1965 the Colombian government made Laguna de Gautavita a national monument, putting it off-limits to gold seekers. Many visitors make a day trip to the lake from nearby Bogotá.

LAS BÓVEDAS These dungeons in Cartagena were constructed in the late 1700s alongside the stone ramparts that protected the city from pirates. The dungeons have served as barracks, as storage facilities and, of course, as a jail.

MUSEO DEL ORO (GOLD MUSEUM) The largest collection of gold works in the world is found in this Bogotá museum. With more than thirty thousand pieces in its collection, the museum displays many rare finds from Colombia's indigenous groups, as well as a wide variety of artifacts in stone, clay, bone, and textiles.

PARQUE NACIONAL DEL CAFÉ (NATIONAL COFFEE PARK) Near the town of Montenegro in Quindio Department, this park includes a museum where visitors can learn about the history of coffee in Colombia and examine machinery used in coffee production.

PARQUE NACIONAL TAYRONA This extensive natural preserve includes deserts, rain forests, and secluded coves and beaches along the coast of the Caribbean Sea. The park also holds the remains of a prehistoric Tayrona village, Pueblito.

audiencia: a Spanish colonial authority with judicial, lawmaking, and administrative powers

barrio: a city district or area. In Colombia, the term *barrios populares* refers to the areas of a city where poor workers live and migrants from the countryside have settled.

bogotazo: the riot that devastated Bogotá following the assassination of Liberal presidential candidate Jorge Eliecer Gaitán on April 9, 1948

Conservative (Conservador): one of the two major political parties in Colombia. Conservatives tend to be supportive of the military, large property owners, and the Roman Catholic Church. Conservatives are oriented toward rural areas.

criollo: a person of European descent who was born in Colombia. In colonial Colombia, the criollos formed a strong class of landowners and government officials.

decentralization: moving or redistributing power from a central authority or government to regional and local authorities or governments

encomienda: a system enforced by the Spanish conquerors of Colombia in which indigenous tribes were forced to provide land and labor to colonial overlords

guerrilla: independent group or individuals carrying out unofficial warfare, including sabotage

Liberal: one of the two major political parties in Colombia. Liberals tend to favor labor rights, government benefits for the poor, and a more limited influence of the Catholic Church. Liberal candidates draw much of their support from urban areas.

M-19: a rural guerrilla movement founded in Colombia in the early 1970s in protest of government corruption. In the early twenty-first century, M-19 became a mainstream political party.

mestizo: a person of mixed European and indigenous heritage. More than half of Colombia's modern population is mestizo.

paramilitary: a group of citizens armed and organized like a military force. Sometimes paramilitary groups are formed to assist regular army troops. In Colombia the major paramilitary group is the United Self-Defense Forces of Colombia (in Spanish, Autodefensas Unidas de Colombia, or AUC).

vallenato: a popular musical form, which started on the Caribbean coast of Colombia in the early 1900s and is characterized by skillful accordion playing

viceroyalty: a colonial government, under the authority of the Spanish king, which exercises legislative and judicial powers, levies taxes, provides for defense, and rules through appointed local governors and mayors

La Violencia: the period of riots, arson, kidnappings, assassinations, and violence in Colombia that began in 1948 and lasted about a decade, resulting in more than 300,000 deaths

Selected Bibliography

Balderston, Daniel, Mike Gonzalez, and Ana López. *Encyclopedia of Contemporary Latin American and Caribbean Cultures.* London: Routledge, 2000.
This three-volume set discusses the leading artists and artistic movements in Latin America, covering music, literature, and visual arts.

Betancourt, Ingrid. *Until Death Do Us Part: My Struggle to Reclaim Colombia.* New York: Ecco Press, 2001.
The Colombian legislator and 2002 presidential candidate describes her experience of political intrigue and corruption and the government's struggle against Colombia's powerful drug cartels.

Bushnell, David. *The Making of Modern Colombia: A Nation in Spite of Itself.* Berkeley: University of California Press, 1993.
The first general history of Colombia written in English, this book covers Colombian culture, history, and modern political developments.

CIA: The World Factbook: Colombia. N.d.
Website: <http://www.cia.gov/publications/factbook/geos/co.html> (September 9, 2003).
This site includes updated statistics on Colombia's population, economy, communications, transportation, military, and transnational issues.

Dydynski, Krzystof. *Colombia.* Lonely Planet Travel Survival Kit Series. Oakland, CA: Lonely Planet Publications, 1995.
A traveler's guide to the country and customs of Colombia, with a useful background on Colombian history and many detailed short articles on Colombian cities, arts and crafts, indigenous peoples, sports, food, and music.

Hanratty, Dennis, and Sandra W. Meditz, eds. *Colombia: A Country Study.* 4th ed. Area Handbook Series. Washington, DC: Government Printing Office, 1990.
This detailed manual, prepared for researchers, U.S. diplomats, and other government personnel stationed in Colombia, includes sections on history, economy, culture, and political affairs.

Kapiszewski, Diana, ed. *Encyclopedia of Latin American Politics: Colombia.* Westport, CT: Oryx Press, 2002.
A comprehensive guide includes entries on past and present political parties, movements, and figures in Latin America.

Library of Congress. *Colombia: A Country Study.* N.d.
Website: < http://lcweb2.loc.gov/frd/cs/cotoc.html> (September 9, 2003).
Using a clear outline format, this site offers useful and succinct information on Colombian history, society, economic affairs, health and welfare, government and politics, and national security.

Pollard, Peter. *Footprint Colombia Handbook: The Travel Guide.* Lincolnwood, IL: Passport Books, 1998.
A general guide to modern Colombia includes useful sections on little-known or out-of-the-way places that most visitors miss.

Population Reference Bureau. **N.d.**
Website: <http://www.prb.org> (September 9, 2003)
This site offers the latest statistics on population trends, fertility and literacy rates, life expectancy, health, and other vital indicators of nations around the world, including Colombia.

Statistical Abstract of the World. **4th ed. Detroit, MI: Gale Group, 2003.**
This reference provides statistics on population, geography, health, education, economics, military affairs, and human rights issues, broken down by country.

United Nations. **N.d.**
Website: <http://www.awww.un.org> (September 9, 2003).
The official site of the United Nations offers updated news briefings as well as a comprehensive section on various current issues, such as refugees, climate change, and human rights in many nations, including Colombia.

Williams, Raymond L., and Kevin G. Guerrieri. *Culture and Customs of Colombia.* Culture and Customs of Latin America and the Caribbean Series. Westport, CT: Greenwood Publishing Group, 1999.
This general review of Colombian history, culture, religion, and politics also has chapters on performing and visual arts.

Cameron, Sara. *Out of War: True Stories from the Front Lines of the Children's Movement for Peace in Colombia.* **New York: Scholastic, 2001.**
The nine stories in this collection are about Colombian teenagers dealing with their nation's guerrilla wars, and the Children's Peace Movement, an organization that seeks to combat the violence.

Carrigan, Ana. *The Palace of Justice: A Colombian Tragedy.* **New York: Four Walls Eight Windows, 1993.**
The author recounts the siege of the Palace of Justice in Bogotá, carried out in 1985 by the guerrilla group M-19.

Diego, Ximena, and Francheska Farinacci, trans. *Shakira: Woman Full of Grace.* **New York: Fireside Books, 2001.**
This biography tells the story of Colombian sensation Shakira, one of the best-selling female vocalists from Latin America, who recorded her first album at age fourteen and has starred on Colombian television.

Eagen, James. *The Aymará of South America.* **Minneapolis: Lerner Publications Company, 2002.**
Explore the traditions of this indigenous group that inhabits Colombia and neighboring countries.

Embassy of Colombia
Website: <http://www.colombiaemb.org> **(September 9, 2003)**
This site includes news reports from U.S. and Colombian sources, pages on arts and culture, and travel and tourism information. A Homework Helper offers statistics and background information for students and researchers.

García Márquez, Gabriel. *Love in the Time of Cholera.* **New York: Alfred A. Knopf, 1988.**
This novel by the acclaimed author of *One Hundred Years of Solitude* is a love story set on the Caribbean coast of Colombia.

Horner, Jeremy. *The Life of Colombia.* **Bogotá: Villegas Editores, 2001.**
The author, an English photographer, depicts Colombian society through a series of 250 color photographs, with text by Colombian writer Gustavo Wilches-Chau.

Katz, Samuel M. *Raging Within: Ideological Terrorism.* **Minneapolis: Lerner Publications Company, 2003.**
Learn about FARC and other South American guerrilla groups.

Márquez, Herón. *Latin Sensations.* **Minneapolis: Lerner Publications Company, 2001.**
Chart the rise of Latin pop stars, including Colombian singer Shakira.

Mutis, Álvaro. *The Adventures and Misadventures of Maqroll.* **Translated by Edith Grossman. New York: New York Review of Books, 2002.**
Seven stories recount the adventures of Maqroll, or "the Lookout." Many critics compare Mutis's stories to the novellas of British writer Joseph Conrad.

Further Reading and Websites

Parnell, Helga. *Cooking the South American Way.* **Minneapolis: Lerner Publications Company, 2003.**
This collection of recipes from South America includes low-fat and vegetarian dishes and provides information about the land, history, people, and cuisines of South America.

vgsbooks.com
Website: <http://www.vgsbooks.com>
Visit vgsbooks.com, the home page of the Visual Geography Series, which is updated regularly. You can get linked to all sorts of useful online information, including geographical, historical, demographic, cultural, and economic websites. The vgsbooks.com site is a great resource for late-breaking news and statistics.

Villegas, Benjamín, Gloria Mercedes Duque, Hans Doring, and Antonio Montana. *The Taste of Colombia.* **New York: St. Martin's Press, 2001.**
A richly illustrated collection of more than one hundred Colombian recipes reveals the varied influences—Spanish, Indian, and African—on Colombian cooking.

Von Rothkirch, Cristóbal, Juan Pablo Ruiz, and Carlos Mauricio Vega. *Alta Colombia: The Splendor of the Mountains.* **New York: St. Martin's Press, 1997.**
A stunning collection of photographs shows the beauty of the Andes Mountains in Colombia.

Captions for photos appearing on cover and chapter openers:

Cover: Coffee plants dot the hills and valleys of west-central Colombia, an area known as the coffee zone.

pp. 4–5 A crop of coffee beans awaits harvest. Coffee historically has been Colombia's most important export.

pp. 8–9 Lush rain forests, like this one in northeastern Colombia, are one of many types of terrain in Colombia.

pp. 20–21 The crumbling buildings of La Ciudad Perdida, or "the lost city," were discovered in 1975. This city was once a major Tayrona settlement.

pp. 36–37 A group of Colombian cowboys in the eastern Llanos watch as their cattle are branded in the corral.

pp. 44–45 A painting by Fernando Botero depicts a schoolgirl reading on a sofa. Botero's signature style features people and animals who are almost comically large and puffy.

pp. 56–57 Colombia's national currency is the peso.

Photo Acknowledgments
The images in this book are used with the permission of: © Victor Englebert, pp. 4-5, 8-9, 10 (both), 13, 14 (top), 15, 18, 19, 20-21, 22, 36-37, 38, 39, 41, 42, 46, 47 (both), 48, 50, 51, 54, 55, 58 (top), 59, 61, 62, 63, 64; Digital Cartographics, pp. 6, 11; © Robert M. Peck/Visuals Unlimited, p. 14 (bottom); © Eugene G. Schulz, pp. 16-17, 17 (bottom), 53; Musée Royal de L'Afrique Centrale, p. 24; © CORBIS, pp. 25, 30; The Art Archive/Eileen Tweedy, p. 27; The Art Archive/Museo Nacional Bogota/Dagli Orti, p. 28; AP/Wide World Photos, pp. 33, 52; © Reuters NewMedia Inc./CORBIS, p. 34; Organization of American States, pp. 44-45; © R. Grazioli/CORBIS SYGMA, p. 49; © Todd Strand/IPS, pp. 56-57, 68; © Jeremy Horner/CORBIS, pp, 58 (bottom), 60; Laura Westlund, p. 69.

Cover photo: © Enzo & Paolo Ragazzini/CORBIS. Back cover photo: NASA.